The best guide of

Samos

with 140 coloured photographs

ATHENS

Publisher:
Stelios Kontaratos
Iakovos Kontaratos
Texts:
Daskalaki Eleni
Photographs:
L. Chapsis, G. Vdokakis, P. Voukouris
A. Rodopoulos, K.Kondos
Artistic Editing:
N. Vagias
Translation:
Avraam Loucaides - A-Z Services
Maps - Townplans:
Airplane editions

32 AEROPIS STR. 118 52 ATHENS
TEL.: (210) 34.50.471 FAX: (210) 34.59.114

ISBN: 960-7439-31-7

Samos

The best guide with 140 coloured photographs

HISTORY - CIVILIZATION - ARTS
FOLKLORE - EXCURSIONS - ROAD MAPS

CONTENTS

8 History

Mythology – History - Pre-historical period of antiquity - The period of acme Pythagoras - Athenians and Spartians Hellenistic and Roman Years - Recent Years

21 Folklore and Traditions

Feasts and Festivals
Holiday Customs

30 Samos & Vathy

Getting to know the town

94 Excursions from Samos

Samiopoula - Tsopela - Kyriakou
Gaidouronissi

98 Ikaria

103 Fourni

104 Ephesus

1st Route 38

Vathy - Gangos - Ag. Paraskevi
Zoodochos Pigi - Ag. Zoni
Psili Ammos

2nd Route 46

Samos - Kokkari - Vourliotes
Moni Vrontianis - Platanakia
Manolates - Stavrinides - Ambelos

3rd Route 56

Karlovasi - Potamos
Seitani - Prophitis Ilias
Pythagora's Cave

4th Route 68

Vathy - Mytilinii - Pythagorio
Eupalinos Tunnel - Monastery of
the Panagia Spiliani - Heraion

5th Route 82

Pythagorio - Mavratzei - Pyrgos
Marathokambos - Spatharei
Pagondas

29: Twon plan
71: Pythagorio plan
108: Geographical map
110: Hotels
112: Useful informations

SAMOS CRUISES

Introduction

The ship arrives at dawn in the port of Vathy on Samos. The old aristocratic houses along the sea-front glow under the first rays of the sun... The sea glitters as it greets the new day that is arriving... The town gradually begins to wake up and prepares to welcome another hot summer day...

We, as awed visitors to this remote island in the Aegean, look at Samos for the first time with a smile on our faces. This green-covered island has won our hearts from the first moment.

In some manner this is exactly how we felt when we collected the information for this guide that you are now holding in your hands. We travelled across Samos from one side of the island to the other, swimming in its crystal-clear waters, climbing up the sides of Kerkis, worshipping piously in the mystagogic atmosphere of the monasteries and the sacred caves of the island.

A small dose of history, a brief journey into the folkloric and rich popular traditions of the Samians and a brief excursion into the secret and visible beauties of Samos are that which are included in our book.

We wish you a pleasant stay and have a good time on this green-filled gem of the Northern Aegean.

Have a wonderful holiday!

Samos through the eons

We often come across Samos in various reports in ancient texts that cover large chronological and historical periods. Other than its present name, we meet it as Anthemis or Anthemousa (probably from the many flowers that grow in its fertile soil), Phyllis (from the many trees that shed their leaves), Dryousa (from the oaks, the acorns that cover the island's hills), Parthenoaroussa (as Hera's choice for her sanctuary). Other names that were also associated with Samos in the past were Doryssa, Melamphyllos, Stefani and Kyparissia.

Exhibit from the Palaeontology Museum

Mythology

According to mythology, **Naiads** or water nymphs lived on Samos during the prehistoric years, wild beasts that gave out terrible roars, which moved the earth and Samos appeared.
The Naiads are the bridges that transport us from mythology to scientific reality. Animal bones millions of years old that were discovered in excavations in the **"Stephanidi"** gorge near the village of **Mytilinii** verify the fact that large prehistoric animals passed from the Asia Minor continent to Samos where they were eventually trapped when Samos split off from the mainland.
These animals that were found on Samos and nowhere else were called "Samothiria" (Samian animals). You can see parts of their skeletons and bones as well as other impressive exhibits in the Palaeontology Museum in Mytilinii.
Even since ancient time Samos has been producing its "Muscat wine", a sweet wine that is enjoyed by the locals and which is the basis the for their trading. But how did grape cultivation reach faraway Samos?
Once upon a time, the god of wine, Dionysos, was chasing the Amazons, who to escape him took refuge on Samos. The inhabitants of the island helped Dionysos, who eventually exterminated them and the site of the battle was named Panaimos (much blood) from the quantity of blood that was spilled there.
In order to reciprocate the help given to him by the Samians, Dionysos gave them the climate that produces this exquisite wine and taught them how

Assyrian bronze statue

Kores (560 B.C.)
Samos
Archaeological
Museum

to make it. Thus, thanks to Dionysos and the Amazons, we are today tasting this sweet Muscat wine made on Samos.

History

The first settlers on the island were discovered in Pythagorio and in the region of Heraion, where during the second millennium B.C. the worshipping of Hera thrived, the most significant of the female deities of Olympus.
The greatest acme experienced by Samos was in the 7th Century B.C. with the founding of many settlements and the island became a significant cultural centre in the 6th Century B.C., while its shipyards built a new type of ship with 50 oars called **"Samaina".**
After the death of the tyrant Polycrates, this bright period began to wane and decline set in. Let us however look at some of the key points in the evolution of Samos in more detail, as well as its history through the passing of time.

PRE-HISTORICAL PERIOD - PERIOD OF ANTIQUITY

The first mythical king of Samos was Angaios, son of the nymph Astypalaias and Apollo, god of light and music. The first settlers on the island were the ancient tribes of the **Chisieon** and the **Astypalaeon,** who lived peacefully on Samos with the passing of time the island was divided into three large districts: Astypalea, Chisia and Aischronia.

The first verified settlers on Samos were considered to be the **Phoenicians,** who according to one theory were the 'god-parents' since in Phoenician the word "sama" means something high. The Phoenicians were soon followed by the Leleges and the Kares (around 1530 B.C.). After the crushing of Minoan Crete (around 1400 B.C.), who contested the supremacy in the Aegean, the Leleges settled on the island through their king Angaio, who was a descendant from Sami in Cephalonia and who had taken part in the Argonaut's quest for the Golden Fleece. Another version as to the derivation of the island's name is based on Angaios' origins from Sami.

Following the laws of evolution and balance of powers, the Leleges were in turn displaced by the **Ionians,** who after many years of battles around 900 B.C. managed to completely dominate the Greeks living on the islands in the Northern Aegean.

The "Samaina"

A plethora of ships were constructed in the shipyards of Samos that took part in many decisive naval battles in the ancient world. The ingenuity of the Samians created a characteristically new type of ship that was called the "Samaina" in honour of Samos. The Samaina combined a spacious hold with the transportation of goods at high speed - a combination that ensured its construction. The Samaina was two-tiered with 50 oars.

Archaeological findings in Heraion

THE PERIOD OF ACME

Samos reached its peak of acme around 550 B.C. under the rule of the tyrant Polycrates. According to Herodotus (the so-called "Father of History") Samos became **the first city of all - Greek and Barbarian or foreign.**

In 532 B.C. Samos became the epicentre of the Ionians through its industrial, trading and nautical activities.

The economic develop-ment of the island also contributed to its cultural development. Polycrates, being a clever and ambi-tious person, managed to

Eupalinos Tunnel

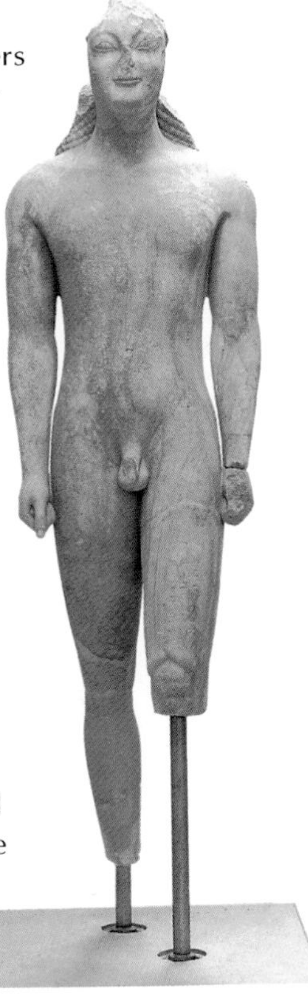

take over power with his brothers Pantagnotus and Syloson and they became tyrants of Samos in 550 B.C. His agreement with his brothers was to divide the island into three sections: Astypalea (which he kept for himself), Chisia and Aischronia (which he gave to his brothers). Later however, he killed his one brother and ousted the other, thus taking over the whole island.
Arts and sciences flourished and the palace of the tyrant Polycrates was transformed into a significant cultural centre. Doctors, poets and philosophers concentrated there, exchanging views and thus enriched their already significant knowledge.
At the same time large architectural works laid the foundations for the period of prosperity that the island enjoyed. The **Eupalinos tunnel** was opened, **the "Iera** Odos" (Sacred Road) was created from Pythagorio to Heraion, the **new Sanctuary dedicated to Hera** was built at the ancient site of worship at Heraion, while Polycrates developed the foundations of the philosophical theory that **"Numbers are the principle of being"**.
In order to solidify his supremacy, Polycrates sought friendly relations with the Egyptian king Amasis, and formed alliances with the Athenian king Peisistratus and with (Lygdamis,) king of Naxos, which finally resulted in his complete dominance of not only the Aegean, but also of a large part of Asia Minor.
Polycrates invited the great architect from Megara, Eupalinos, to Samos to construct an aqueduct to carry water from one side of the mountain to the

Pythagorio Monument (1989) by Nikolaos Ikaros

other. The **aqueduct** that was constructed was a unique achievement for that period.

Dug in the depths of the Kastro (or Kastri) Mountain -at a depth of 80 meters from its peak- the aqueduct had a length of 1,046 m. The tunnel was opened concurrently at both sides of the mountain and the two subterranean diggings met at the middle with only a few meters difference.

Other than the ceramic pipes, the width and height of the tunnel also allowed access by people, which indicated that the tunnel was also used as a secret passageway in case the city was besieged.

Other than being a good soldier and an intelligent

administrator, Polycrates was admittedly a very lucky person. When King Amasis of Egypt was informed of the rumours of his luck, he wrote to his ally saying that the great invocation of luck provokes envy of both gods and man and the king then advised him to create a sorrowful incident for himself in order to minimise this envy.
Listening to this advise, Polycra-tes threw one of his most precious and loved rings into the sea - a ring that he never took off his finger. A few days later the palace's cook found the ring in the stomach of a large fish that he was preparing for Polycrates and returned it to him.
When Amasis learnt this, he predicted that Polycrates' end would be as bad as his life had been, and this is what hap-pened. Polycrates was tricked and captured by the Persian satrap in Sardeis and crucified in 552 B.C.
Other works that were constructed during the period of Polycrates' tyranny were the walls surrounding the city (a length of 6,200 meters) and the naval port of Pythagorio.

Pythagoras

One of the greatest mathema-ticians in antiquity who also achieved fame in philosophy and music. Born on Samos between 580 and 576 B.C. his parents were Mni-sarchos and Pythaida.
As a small child Pythagoras studied under several great scientists, including **Ferekides** from Lesvos, **Ermodamantis** from Samos and **Thalis** and **Anaximandros** from Mylito. Growing up, he was accepted at the court of the Egyptian Pharaoh

Amasis and the higher priesthood of Mefidas. During this period he was initiated into the Egyptian sacraments.
Later, as a prisoner of the Persians he was taken to Babylon where he had the opportunity to complete his knowledge through his associa-tions with Persian wizards and learned persons.
Returning to Samos, Pytha-goras came into conflict with the tyrannical regime of Poly-crates and was forced to leave again. His wanderings guided him to Krotona in Lower Italy where he formed a philosophical school which is considered to be the first university in the world.

Pythagoras' philosophy was closely related to numbers. According to him, the principle and essence of being are numbers. Pythagoras named the universe "world" (gem) due to the harmony that governs it.
In the field of Mathematics, the Pythagorean Theory has been accepted throughout the world as the basis to Mathematics. According to this Theory, the square of the length of the hypotenuse of a right-angled triangle equals the sum of the squares of the lengths of the other two sides or
$(AC)2 = (AB)2 + (BC)2$.
Another innovation of Pythagoras was the multiplication table that gives the product of the first ten whole numbers.
Pythagoras died in Krotona in Lower Italy around 500 B.C. but his heritage lives on even today in the scientific world.

ATHENIANS AND SPARTANS

The domination of Samos after Polycrates reverted back to the **Persians** after quite a few adventures. Among the barbaric acts that were carried out were the burning and destruction of Heraion, which in

Ruins of an Old Christian Basilica

the meantime had collected a multitude of priceless treasures.

After the tyrannical rules of Maeandrius, Syloson, Aiakes and Theomystoras that followed, in September 479 B.C. these long-lasting tyrannies of the island ended at the Battle at Mycale. The Samians allied themselves with the Athenians and the Spartans and were thus able to give the final crushing blow to the Persian army that had sought refuge in the Straits of Mycale after they had been defeated in the naval battle at Salamina.

Samos, together with the other autonomous States, became a members of the Athenian League headed by the Athenians. The Samians paid a tribute -as did all the members of the League- to the common fund of Dilos and gradually with the passing of time they regained their powers and managed to re-create a powerful navy.

War broke out between Athens and Samos because of the former's demand that the Allies pay a higher tribute and the latter's refusal to pay this increase. The powerful Athenian State sent its naval

Findings from the Old Basilica in Pythagorio

force headed by Admiral Pericles to attack Samos in 439 B.C. Athens defeated the Samian Navy and invaded Samos, beginning a nine-month siege of the capital which ended in Athens conquering the island, destroying and looting whatever they came across and forcing the Samians to pay a large tribute while compelling them to re-join the Athenian League.

The island was faithful to Athens during the Peloponnesian War and in recognition of their assistance, the Athenians re-gave the island its independence. But this peace lasted for only a short period of time since the Lacedaemonians - wanting to punish Samians for their new alliance with Athens- besieged and conquered the island, ruling it for a period of about ten years.

HELLENISTIC AND ROMAN YEARS

The **Apostle Paul** was the first person to preach Christianity on Samos in 59. At the same time however, Samos was being continuously raided and looted by the pirates that began to dominate the Aegean during that period, as well as by the German tribes - the Goths, the Huns and the Alaniths.
During the period when the Byzantine lands were being divided into Issues or Themes, Samos belonged to the 16th Theme together with Rhodes and their other neighbouring islands. This Theme was given the honorary name of "Island of Samos". Since the Roman Empire had at this time disintegrated and the Byzantine Empire had extended itself so much it could not defend its lands, Samos came under repeated raids from pirates. In 887 the island fell into the hands of the Saracens until the middle of the 10th Century when it was recaptured from the Byzantines by Nikiphoros Fokas.
When the Franks occupied Constantinople in 1204, Samos passed under the dominance of the Latins. The final demise of the Byzantine Empire also signalled the decline of Samos as its inhabitants left the island, not being able to withstand the continuous raids and looting. These predatory raids supplemented the natural disasters that hit the island, thus adding to the desolation.

RECENT YEARS

The few Samians who remained on the island found refuge on the sides of the inaccessible mountains, hidden from both man and gods. The ruins that you will come across during your

excursions date back to this period.
In 1562 a squadron of the Turkish Navy reached Samos and by chance discovered the few inhabitants that lived on this derelict island. Sultan Suleiman the Legislator was immediately notified, who decreed that the island should be colonised and be exempted from paying any taxes.
During the Greek Revolution of 1821, Samos played a leading role in the uprising with men like Lycourgos Logothetis, Stamatis Georgiadis, Costandis Lachanas, Bishop Cyrillos and other liberation fighters. Their valiant followers were involved in many battles while diversionary attacks along the neighbouring shores of Asia Minor gave hope to the Christians in those regions.
In 1830, through the **"Protocol of London"** and decisions passed by the Allied Powers (England, France, Russia), Samos was excluded from the borders of the newly formed Greek State. The Samians did not accept this new status quo and finally, through continuous battles and assertions they were awarded many privileges. Samos was declared a privileged Turkish district with hegemony by Turkey.
In essence, Samos had a Christian prince who was of course appointed by the Sultan, its own flag, customs, courts and all local matters were resolved by the Samian Parliament. The capital was transferred from Chora to Vathy, the latter developing into a large naval and trading centre.
Despite this, hope and a deep yearning for unification of the island with mother Greece still beat strongly in the hearts of the Samians. On March 2nd 1912 the prince (Andreas Kopasis) who had been appointed by the Turks was murdered and on November 11th of the same year, the Samian National Assembly led by Themistoklis Sofoulis, ended this form of government and declared the **"Union of Samos with the Free Greek Kingdom".** The official union was cele-

brated on March 2nd 1913.
From that moment began the rebirth of Samos and its common progress with the rest of Greece. After many battles -which we mention only a few in this book-, Samos today has managed to achieve significant development and in recent years the island has entered dynamically into the tourist sector, which is one of the largest economic activities in our country.

Folklore and Traditions

The many-faceted island of Samos has many beautiful spots to offer its visitors who have the urge to wander around and explore its hidden niches. Whether you are in the small or large villages that are situated along the coast or in the hills, the churches or the monasteries with their local festivals, you will come across local popular art and traditions that are still alive and vibrant.
Ceramics is one of the more renowned works of art found on Samos. Crafted with especial technique and artistry, their originality and uniqueness immediately makes them the number one selection for the visitor. The villages of Mavratzei and Koumaradei are among the older ceramic centres

Ceramics having symbolic value

on the island, while Vathy and Karlovasi had large workshops in the past.
Among the cups and jars, bowls and other ornamental objects, two singular vessels stand out: the "**masked bartak**" and the "**just cup**". In order to drink water from the masked bartak, you must know about the 'secret' holes that you must close with your fingers, otherwise the water will dribble on you. As for the just cup, this is a measure against greediness! If you try to fill the cup over the marked level, the water will dribble out of a hole in the base of the cup. If of course you restrain yourself, you will be able to enjoy your cool water.
Certain remains from leather-processing or tanning workshops still stand out once you reach Karlovasi, an art that was well-known to the locals and who practised it with zeal in the past.
Another product that was renowned and still continues today to be renowned is hand-woven finely-detailed textiles and materials. The village of Marathokambos produced many skilled weavers and embroideresses. With its named "bibilas", Samian lace is renowned for its finely detailed workmanship and successful combinations. Using a special technique, the weavers of Marathokambos spun sheep's wool into carpets and bags.

FEASTS AND FESTIVALS

Holidays and festivals are a part of every significant moment of the small agricultural community of the old Samos. Births, baptisms, local and religious holidays... all give joy to the whole village. All together in moments of joy, as in moments of sadness - this is the reality of everyday life.
Festivals create a great opportunity for holding a feast in the village and the greater community in gene-ral, in the sense of a purely collective cha-racter. The participa-tion of every family in the preparations of the festival is almost obligatory. Even expa-triates return to the village to renew their ties with their fellow-villagers and their birth-place.
The organisation of and participation in the festivities are based on old customs. The dances and songs, the position in the circle where each reveller will dance in

A loom in the Folkloric Museum

accordance with his/her age and social standing is known to everyone.

"The only musical organ used in the dancing is the "tsambouna" (bagpipes), without the "toumbe-rleki" (oblong folk drum) or the "daouli" (tabor). A boy dances in front -the "kavous"- followed by the girls and finally by a boy again - the "petala". A boy cannot join the middle of the dance; only the bridegroom is allowed to during the festivities of the wedding.

The "tsambouniaris" (bagpiper) stands in the centre of the dance playing the bagpipes. The dance is circular and lively. When the person leading the dance finishes, he puts a couple of coins into the pomponned shoe of the bagpiper.

Traditional Samian clothing

The dance with the bagpipes is followed by a "singing" dance, which is preferred because they can dance without paying and because this gives the opportunity to the couples to show their feelings and their longings, even if it is only through lyrics.

Confessions of love, complaints, promises, spirits and broken relationships that were once. The person leading the dance would sing the first lyrical couplet which was repeated by everyone in the dance, as well as by anyone watching the dance. The same happened with each lyric and couplet.

Anyone dancing had the right to say his own couplet. In many cases the song turned into a singing dialogue between two persons in love.

Sometimes the dialogue reached the point where a relationship was broken and this was then followed by contumacious songs that were caustic and indiscriminate".
(Samos Folklore, Volume I, Nikolaos Dimitriou)

HOLIDAY CUSTOMS

On Easter Sunday Marathokambos has an especial atmosphere with the dozens of "balothies" (shots fired into the air) that the locals shoot into the air. The five parishes in the village compete and the result is impressive, if not deafening!
In another village, Spathareous, the custom of the "Cadi" is carried out even today, which is a satirical trial-parody of the Cadi (Turkish judge) during the

Folkloric museum Dorissa Bay

Turkish occupation period. Going from house to house, the people accompanying the Cadi are treated to raki, tsipouro and wine. When they finally end up at the courthouse where the Cadi will judge, the moment of ridicule arrives and the Cadi is "hung".
Similar festivities with masked persons also take place in Marathokambos during carnival time - the so-called "fratzolia" which is a combination of popular festivities and carnival carousal.

Excursions

The island of the famous mathematician and sculpture Pythagoras greets its visitors arriving at its port at the bottom of a cove that is well-sheltered from the wind. This is where the capital of Samos is situated, now united with the traditional settlement of Vathy. The second port of the island, Karlovasi, services mainly those visitors headed for the south-western part of Samos.

The ships sail close to the beaches during the last mile or so before reaching Samos. The villages with their red roofs can barely be seen among the tall trees. Behind the village houses stands the peak of Kerkis, the highest mountain in the Aegean, which offers those arriving by air -as well as to those more daring hikers- a fantastic view of the islands of the Cyclades and the Dodecanese.

Samos is covered with thick forests which have decreased over recent years due to forest-fires and which include olive trees, citrus trees and endless vine-yards which produce the famous Samian wine. The shores of the island are covered with small pebbles and sand, washed by translucent icy waters.

We can clearly discern the shores of Asia Minor a stone's-throw away from the eastern section of Samos . This short distance that separates two different civilisations always brought Samos to the forefront since many races tried to conquer the island.

However, Samos always resisted and developed its civilisation by bearing persons who were destined to enrich scientific knowledge and to beautify this world of ours through their art; People like **Pythagoras,** a great mathematician and philosopher, the astronomer **Aristarchos,** the sculpture **Roikos** and his son Theodoros, **Eupalinos from Megara** who constructed the renowned aqueduct in Pythagorio and Pythagoras the sculpture, are just some of the great personalities who were born or who lived on Samos.

ΣΑΜΟΣ
SAMOS

■	ΤΡΑΠΕΖΑ	BANK
1.	ΑΣΤΥΝΟΜΙΑ	POLICE
2.	ΤΑΧΥΔΡΟΜΕΙΟ	POST OFFICE
3.	ΛΙΜΕΝΑΡΧΕΙΟ	PORT AUTHORITY
4.	ΔΗΜΑΡΧΕΙΟ	TOWN HALL
5.	ΝΟΜΑΡΧΙΑ	PREFECTURE
6.	ΑΡΧΑΙΟΛΟΓΙΚΟ ΜΟΥΣΕΙΟ	ARGHEOLOGICAL MUSEUM
7.	ΒΥΖΑΝΤΙΝΟ ΜΟΥΣΕΙΟ	BYZANTINE MUSEUM
8.	ΔΗΜΟΣΙΑ ΒΙΒΛΙΟΘΗΚΗ	PUBLIC LIBRARY
9.	Κ.Τ.Ε.Λ.	BUS STATION
10.	ΤΑΞΙ	TAXI
11.	ΠΛΑΤΕΙΑ ΠΥΘΑΓΟΡΑ	PITHAGORAS SQUARE
12.	ΠΛΑΤΕΙΑ ΑΓ. ΝΙΚΟΛΑΟΥ	AG. NIKOLAOS SQUARE

N
W
E
S

ΘΕΜΙΣΤΟΚΛΗ ΣΟΦΟΥΛΗ - THEMISTOKLI SOFOULI

ΛΥΚΟΥΡΓΟΥ ΛΟΓΟΘΕΤΗ - LYKOURGOU LOGOTHETI

PARKING

O.T.E.

ΚΑΡΛΟΒΑΣΙ - ΠΥΘΑΓΟΡΕΙΟ
KARLOVASI - PITHAGORIO

SAMOS AND VATHY

Let us begin our tour of Samos with the town and port that has the same name. **Samos or Vathy** has been the capital of the island since 1832, the latter being the main port of Samos, together with Karlovasi. During the last century the port was a small community that was created by the traders from Vathy in order to offer better services, and with time the two settlements joined to become the beautiful island town that we see when we first arrive on Samos.

The neo-classical buildings and old mansions bear witness to the former economic might of the island. Travelling along the sea-front we come across **Pythagoras Square** with its marble lion. Standing out in the background are the blue domes of the **Church of Ag. Spyridona** and a little further down the **old Parliament** with the **Town Hall** and the **Art Gallery.** You can visit the **Archaeological Museum** that is situated next to the Town Hall and a small distance away is the Ecclesiastical-Byzantine Museum. The Archaeological Museum is housed in two buildings: the first building is the actual museum while the second is the **Paschalio Library**.

Panoramic view of the town of Samos

Pythagoras Square in Vathy and the coastal road

For this reason keep your ticket for the Museum because you will be asked for it when you want to enter the second building.
The findings that are exhibited in the first hall of the Archaeological Museum are derived mainly from Heraion and "Iera Odos" (Sacred Road) that linked the ancient town -which was sited where Pythagorio now stands- with Heraion.
The most significant exhibit is the colossal **statue of a "kouros"** (youth) from Heraion. The body was discovered in 1980 in excavations along the Sacred Road. Other parts of the statue were discovered in stages, thus gradually showing the grandeur of the form of the statue. The first part to be found was the left thigh, followed by the body of the statue and finally in 1984, its face. The kouros was the work of a Samian artist, sculptured from Samian marble with ash-white streaks.
In its initial form the kouros was painted with chestnut-red ocra, while various details such as the hair, eyes, lips and public hair stood out with other colours. Even though today we consider it strange and unusual, the ancient artists usually painted their creations so as to be more like reality.
The initial height of the kouros was estimated to be 4.75 m. By carefully measuring the complete form it was obvious that the external dimensions as well as the proportions of the members of the body of the statue were based on a metric system whose basic unit was the ancient Samian "pichi" (52.3 cm).

"Kouros", one of the most significant findings in the Archaeological Museum

The second section of the Museum is housed in the Paschalio Library, which houses the findings from the excavations that have been carried out over the years in different parts of the island. Other than the impressive findings -keep a look-out for the many giffins, the mythical birds of Hera- of interest are also the descriptive articles that we can read and which brings us into contact with the daily routines in antiquity, and especially on Samos.
The Byzantine Museum also does not lack in the

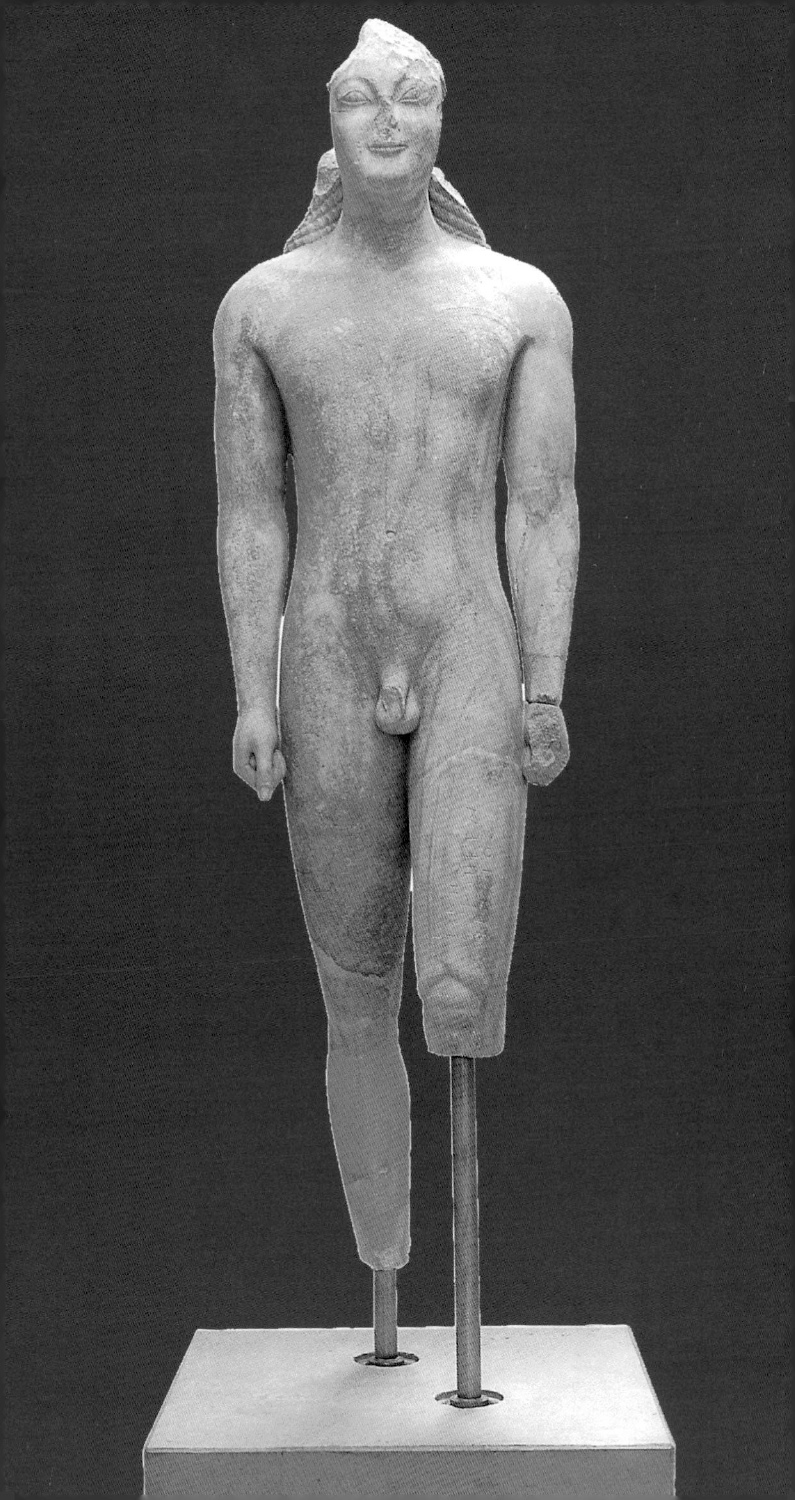

number and significance of its exhibited artefacts. The majority of these have been collected from the monasteries and old churches found on the island and among the items that you can see are modest Post-Byzantine icons, gold chalices, valuable manuscripts and historical mementoes, rare books and Bibles.
Take a stroll through the small roads behind the main road of the port **-Sofoulis Avenue-** where the Samian market is situated. If you feel like walking, follow the coastal road past the port towards the hospital where you will be able to admire -other than the view of

A traditional shop in the town

Samos and the picturesque closed cove- some of the more grand mansions on the island.
Our second proposal for your walk is to the traditional settlement of Vathy, to the old village that is perched on the hill overlooking the port. Here you will feel as if time is running backwards.
The little narrow uphill alleys with their parapets, the small stone houses with their spotless doorsteps and neat yards, some impressively carved marble balconies and wooden roofed verandas - all blend together to re-awake memories in the elderly and to show the young some aspects of the recent past of life in our country.

36-37. The picturesque town of Samos with its little harbour

Uphill roads and stone houses bring back memories of other eras in Vathy

Vathy - Gangos - Ag. Paraskevi Zoodochos Pigi - Ag. Zoni - Psili Ammos

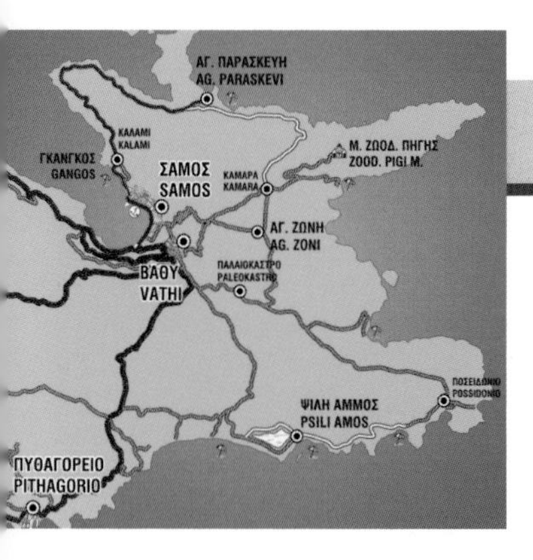

Samos is a large island with many natural beauties and sites which requires both time and disposition to enjoy. But even if your stay on the island is limited, the many possibilities that are offered to you will ready boost your mood. The starting point for our excursions will be Vathy.

So beginning with the eastern part of the island, we will swim along beautiful beaches, we will seek serenity in the two old Monasteries of Zoodochos Pigi and Agia Zoni and we will end up for lunch in the picture-sque nooks of Klima or Poseidonio.

Following the eastward road from the port, after five or ten minutes we can make our first stop at the enchanting and leeward facing **beach of Gangos** with its large pebbles and clear waters, which invite us to dive in. Just above the beach are a few hotels and tavernas where we can enjoy a vacation day without being bothered with cars and kilometres. Carrying on east-wards we end up at the picture-sque cove of Ag. Paraskevi with the church of the same name.

To continue our exploration we will have to return

The beautiful beach at Gangos

Entrance to the Monastery of Zoodochos Pigi

to Vathy and take the road leading to Zoodochos Pigi, where we will come to a fork in the road which terminates at **Vlamari.** Situated here are the very old ruins of the Church of Agia Zoni. In 1695 a faithful monk was aided by the local residents in building a new church that gradually became a monastery.

It is worth stopping at the monastery to admire the wall murals dating back to the 17th C., the wooden iconostasis that was crafted in 1801 as well as the small 19th C. icons that adorn the church.

About 5 km from Vathy is another notable monastery, that of **Zoodochos Pigi of Kotsika.** This monastery took its name in remembrance of the vision of a monk from New Ephesus who around 1730 saw in his sleep an icon of the Virgin

The blue-green waters of Mourtia and Mycale

Scenic fish-tavernas and crystal waters in Poseidonio and Klima

The beach at Psili Ammos is ideal for children

Mary at the roots of a cedar tree (in the local dialect the cedar is called 'kotsika'). When he dug up the roots he actually found the icon and he gradually built a complete monastery around the old church.
The monastery is surrounded by tall pine trees and cypress trees and there is a wonderful pine forest behind the grounds.
Ask the monk for permission to take a stroll in the forest where you will feel as if you are walking on feathers since a thick layer of acorns covered the ground.
At the foot of the monastery lies the **beach of Mourtia.** Covered with greenery, it is perfect for solitary swimming. However, the whole region with its sky blue scenery and unimpeded view is perfect for relaxation and meditation.
One of the most popular beaches on Samos is **Psili Ammos** (fine sand), which is relatively close to Vathy. Just its name will attract our attention since most of the beaches on the island are covered with

The Monastery of Zoodochos Pigi

pebbles, as sand is a rarity here. On this beach you will not find even one pebble, while its shallow and warm waters are ideal for children.

The two charming villages of **Poseidonio** and **Klima** lie just a short distance from Vathy and Pythagorio. They are just a short distance away from Turkey, separated by the Strait of Mycale, while colourful fishing boats lie on cement piers inside the sea.

The Monastery of Agia Zoni

At the fork after **Paleokastro** the road leads us to the attractive beaches at **Kerveli** and **Platanaki.**

After swimming in the cool and refreshing waters you can relax at the local taverna with an enjoyable meal accompanied by local sweet wine.

As for this route, if you do it at night-time, you will be able to see -with mixed feelings- along some of the curves in the road the many lights of the Turkish coastal town of Kusantasi. So near yet so far!

44-45. Kokkari

Samos - Kokkari - Vourliotes Moni Vrontianis - Platanakia Manolates - Stavrinides Ambelos

2nd Route

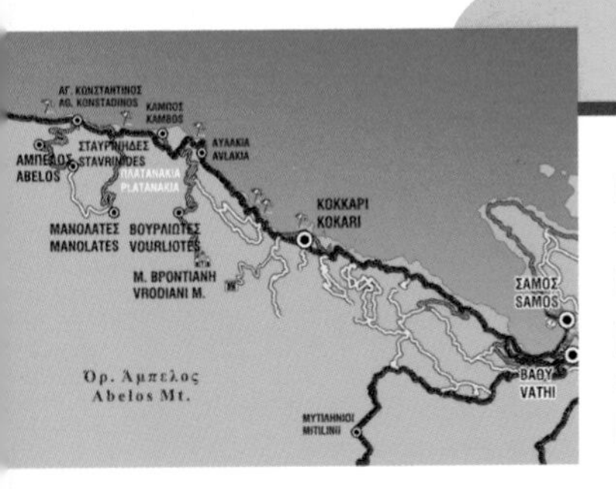

Following the coastal road towards the northern part of the island we will come across little picturesque fishing harbours and tourist centres, exceptional beaches and wonderful scenery. From Pythagoras Square in Vathy we travel along the coastal road and after half a kilometre or so we meet the new road that will take us to **northern Samos.** The major part of this route is next to the sea; once we leave the coast we come across impressive scenery with an orgasm of vegetation, small streams and gullies.

Travelling to Kokkari we will first come across the settlement of **Kedros** and less than 30 minutes from Vathy we enter **Kokkari,** which with its wonderful beaches, graphic tavernas and a selection of proposals to choose from with respect to the night's entertainment, is number one on the visitor's list.

Kokkari is situated on the nose of a small peninsula with its houses perched on the low hill. With a large northward beach and a smaller southward beach the bathers may choose which beach to swim in, depending on the direction of the wind.

The paved coastal road is covered from one end to

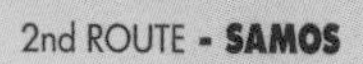

Kokkari attracts a significant number of visitors during the summer period

Crystal waters and virgin land at Lemonakia

the other with tables and multi-coloured chairs. Cafeterias, fish-tavernas, ouzeries, bars and whatever else you may desire during your holidays are at your feet.

We continue heading north-west where one by one we come across the impressive beaches of **Tsamadou, Lemonakia, Veletza** and **Tsambou** - each one more alluring, more inviting, more glittering under the hot rays of the sun!

The attractive beach at Tsambou

Multi-coloured stones and pebbles, crystal-clear waters and virgin land that is pleasantly disturbed by large coloured umbrellas. The smooth dirt roads leading to these beaches are accessible by motorcycles and four-wheel drive vehicles, as well as by the more daring car drivers.

If you are not one of the daring drivers, leave your car on the road and introduce a little adventure into your holidays with a ten-minute descent (and climbing back up later). You may tire yourself a little more but there's no doubt that the scenery will recompense you. And if you're lucky and there is no wind when you descend to the beach, we are sure that you will be enthralled.

After leaving the beaches, drive on a few more kilometres towards the **village of Vourliotes.** **Avlakia** -which you will meet at the junction- is just one more sea-side village with a small tourist infrastructure and hospitable inhabitants. Just after

The cosmopolitan beach at Tsamadou

Avlakia is the settlement of **Kambos.**

Reaching Vourliotes we cannot but notice the terraces where the vineyards are cultivated. Vourliotes is the highest wine-producing village on Samos. An easier and more popular path begins soon after leaving Vourliotes, which ends in Kokkari. The distance is approximately 4 km and the landscape that we pass through is covered with vegetation, while offering a wonderful view.

Stop awhile for an ouzo and a meal in the graphic square in Vourliotes and then continue onto our

next destination, which is the 16th C. **Monastery of the Panagia of Vrontiani.** This Monastery is surrounded by trees and two wells -one of which is inside the courtyard of the Monastery- which adds to the scenery of the region.

The little **"Chapel of Metamorfossi of Sotira"** is beautifully decorated with its Byzantine style and its masterpiece being the finely carved wooden iconostasis.

A large festival is held at the monastery on August 15th and on September 8th (when the Virgin Mary is celebrated) and many of the faithful congregate here. The festivities begin at the village the day before and end at the monastery where the air of devoutness blends with the popular festival. They begin walking along the pathway from **Vrontiani** towards the peak of Karvounis -**Prophitis Ilias**- at a height of 1,153 m while enjoying the enchanting view of the Aegean.

The Temple inside the Monastery

The Monastery of Panagia Vrontiani

Returning to the main road, we again head north-westerly and a few kilometres later we come

across an enchanting area that is perfect for a hike under the tall 'platania' or plane trees, next to running water and rich vegetation. No wonder the area is called **Platanakia.** A hotel and several tavernas offer their hospitality to those who would like to remain longer to enjoy the scenery.
The houses in the village of **Ag. Constantinos** spread out under the green pine trees and here you will find fish tavernas situated on the water,

View from the village of Vourliotes

Conversation, mezedes and good wine in the scenic square of the village

Manolates perched on the mountain inside dense vegetation

Agios Constantinos next to the sea

washed by the waves of the clean waters that disappear into the horizon after the narrow beach. A mountain road, shadowed by the tall plane trees and accompanied by running water which irrigates the thick vegetation, runs parallel to the ravine while climbing up the mountain and leads us to the

villages of **Manolates, Ambelos and Stavrinides**. While journeying to Manolates, it is worth stopping at the **"forest of the nightingales"**, where thousands of these affable birds have built their nests in this so beautiful forest. Especially in May the forest fills with their melodious chirrups, thus creating a true banquet.

A sense of enjoyment can be found in the afternoon in Avlakia

There is a path that leads from Manolates to Stavrinides, offering a panoramic view with the eye hugging the north shores of Samos all the way to Vathy.

On July 20th the memory of Prophitis Ilias is celebrated at Stavrinides with an impressive Samian festival. All visitors are treated to "Giorti", a festivity Samian soup cooked in huge vats and its ingredients include grounded wheat, onions and meat. When the service ends the priest blesses the food and distributes it to the faithful, together with pieces of consecrated bread.

54-55. Sunset in Kokkari

Karlovasi - Potamos Seitani - Prophitis Ilias Pythagora's Cave

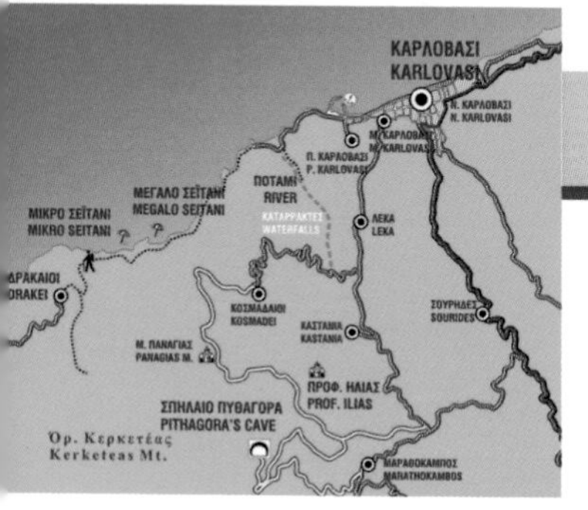

3rd Route

Beginning from Vathy we can stop at **Piaki** beach just before Karlovasi - passing by the junction in the road- for a swim and also visit the mountain **village of Idroussa.**

Karlovasi is the second port as well as the second largest town on Samos after Vathy. Some old mansions, impressive churches and deserted leather processing factories bring back memories of the old glories and economic might that the town once had. Karlovasi is also the birthplace of Lycourgos Logothetis (a hero from the Revolution of 1821) and Kleanthis, a folk singer who fought against the Turkish State. Five old suburbs -or 'Karlovasia' as they are called by the locals- make up Karlovasi: **Palio (old) Karlovasi, Neo (new) Karlovasi, Meseo (middle) Karlovasi, Ormos (bay) and Limani (port).** Just outside Palio Karlovasi is the Monastery of Ag. Ioannis Theologos, built in

A church in Karlovasi

A general view of Karlovasi

1823, while the church is a little older and dates back to the 18th C., and was renovated in 1823 by the Samian Chieftain in the Revolution, Manuel Angelinas. The old icon of Christ that you can admire is an 18th work of art while the temple contains a novel depiction of the Virgin Mary hugging a crucified Jesus.

Travelling south of Karlovasi we come across another old monastery, that of **Prophitis Ilias,** which was built in the 17th C. It contains small remarkable icons, small sections of the first wall murals and a marble slab in the centre of the main chapel, which has inscribed on it a two-eagled cross and the firstly created Adam and Eve - all are just some of the relics you can admire in the chapel. Exhibits from the library of the monastery that stand out are many old manuscripts and sacred books, including a Bible dating back to 1518. Continuing along the road we reach the mountain village of **Konteika.**

Megalo Seitani, a remote and spectacular beach

A few kilometres to the west is the beach at **Potamos** with its smooth pebbles and crystal-clear blue waters, which is considered to be one of the most attractive on Samos. Behind the beach is a green-covered gully and a little

Original and rare architecture can be seen in the Church of Ag. Nikolaos

westwards there are some hot mineral springs. The path that lies behind the beach will lead us to a small paradise.

A small river with a waterfall -depending on the season and winter rainfall- spread out among the thick vegetation. Whoever decides to follow the uphill path along the banks will find before him an idyllic little lake, while a dive in the icy waters will wash away the weariness of the climb.

The forest behind the region of Potamos is ideal for a stroll. Its unique natural beauty is complemented by thousands of butterflies which if you are lucky you may see streaks of colour emitted by their multi-coloured wings shooting into the blue sky near the **little Church of Ag. Paraskevi.**

An accessible dirt road ends up at two remote coves that are shelters for the **Mediterranean seal (monachus monachus)** which live in the transparent waters of the Aegean. These two coves are called **Little Seitani and Big Seitani.**

Karlovasi is ideal as the centre for your excursions to the nearby villages of **Kosmadeous** and **Kastania**

Agia Triada and Myrtidiotissa, two of the many scenic churches found on the island

Blue-green waters, swimming and relaxation along the beaches of Potami and Mikro (small) Seitani - Kataraktis (waterfall), a small paradise

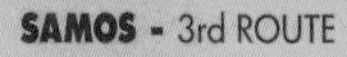

Pythagoras found refuge on Mt. Kerkis

and for hiking along the slopes of Kerkis. The trails begin from Potami and with many branch-offs end up at **Drakeous** (behind Seitani), **Ag. Panteleimona, Plaka** and **Kastania.** These routes are among the most impressive that you can find throughout the mountain pathways of Europe, but in the majority of cases you will need the experience of a professional guide so as not to lose yourself.

About half way heading from Laka towards Kastania you will meet a country road leading to Kosmadeous and from there to the **Monastery of Koimisis tis Theotokou** and the **Cave of Pythagora** (Pythagora's Cave).

This is a cave with a dome-like roof that is hidden among the green slopes of Kerkis. This cave was where Pythagoras hid out with his pupils in order to escape from Polycrates after the philosopher returned from his travels to Egypt and Persia.

According to another version, Pythagora's real cave was in the 'Monastery of the Panagia Spiliani near Pythagorio (see 4th Route). Passing through the **Kakoperato Farangi** (Bad Pass Ravine) -don't let the name frighten you, even though it seems from afar that there is no good path passing through it- you

The Spileo (Cave) and the Church of Sarantaskaliotissa

will reach the **Monastery of Evangelistria** which is surrounded by a wonderful pine forest.
Other than Pythagora's Cave, the eastern slopes of Kerkis also includes the **Cave of Sarantaskaliotissa** (Cave of Forty Steps) with the Chapel of Panagia (Virgin Mary) being built deep in the cave. In order to reach the Chapel we have to climb down 40 steps carved in the stone, hence the name of the cave.
The little villages of Kallithea, **Ag. Kyriaki and**

Plaka Beach

Drakei are nestled on the western slopes of Kerkis and when walking in this region you will discover the ruins of old churches that were build during the 8th C. by Pavlos the Latrinos. Turning left on the road leading to Drakei we arrive in the small village of **Ag. Isidoros,** known for its caique-building yards. **Mt. Kerkis**, the highest mountain on Samos, is criss-crossed by dozens of pathways for hiking. From April to June hundreds of visitors arrive on Samos from abroad in order to explore its secret spots.

Experienced guides-mountaineers are there to bring you into contact with Nature. Most of them are contracted to the travel agencies who bring the tourists directly from other European countries, but you can ask the locals for a guide to accompany you. It is necessary that for your mountain-climbing you wear socks and a pair of stout athletic shoes with a thick sole and high sides, but mountain boots are even better. Wear light clothes but take a warm

66-67. Karlovasi

The village of Ag. Isidoros, known for its caique-building yards

jacket with you because you may come across a lot of humi-dity when you are high up on the mountain. Don't forget your sun-block be-cause during some parts of your hike you will be travel-ling under the sun.

However, the most important fact is that if you do not go with a professional guide, you must notify someone as to the route that you will be taking and be sure to learn about the conditions of the pathway you have chosen.

This is a must because after the winter rains it is possible that one of the small bridges may have been destroyed or the pathway may be damaged, thus causing you to change your route.

Whatever you do, the fascination of the moun-tain, the ever-changing scenery and the fantastic view that you will enjoy will surely recompense you for the weariness you may feel after your hike.

The picturesque village of Kallithea

Vathy - Mytilinii - Pythagorio Eupalinos Tunnel - Monastery of the Panagia Spiliani Heraion

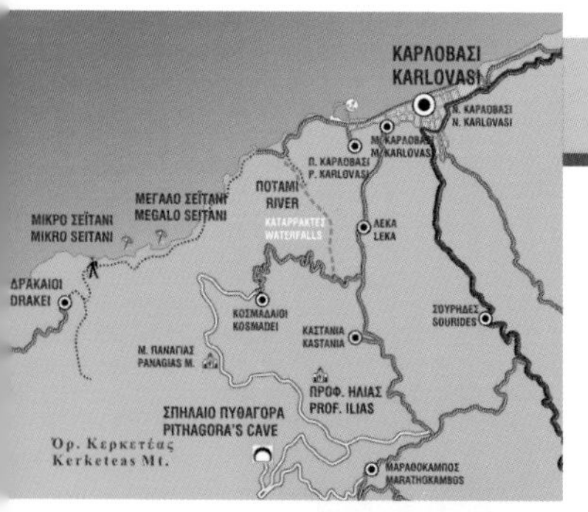

This is one more trip that starts from Vathy or alternatively, you can stay in Pythagorio which is - together with Kokkari- the most famous areas on Samos, and from here you can explore the southern part of the island.

On the road to Pythagorio we make a small detour to the village of **Mytilinii** where unique fossilised animals that lived in the region 8-10 million years ago were discovered. But the most impressive are those artefacts exhibited at the **Aegean Palaeontology and Physical Museum** that is housed in a neat modern building situated on the outskirts of the village. Among the exhibitions that stand out is the stuffed cat-like animal that lived more than 200 years ago on the island and known as the **'Kaplani of Samos'.**

An up and coming tourist region is the beach at **Glykorizo** just before Pythagorio. In addition, a signpost just outside Pythagorio guides us to the **archaeological site at Thermes,** which is a Roman

Ceramic roofs and little narrow roads depict the village of Mytilinii

Bath. Excavations carried out by the German Archaeological Society brought to light the greatest part of the installations, the foundations of buildings and walls that have been preserved up to a significant height.

The current Pythagorio is situated on the same site as the ancient town of Samos. Its port bustles with activity with the daily arrival of sailboats and excursion vessels. From here trips are organised to the nearby islands and to Kusantasi on the Turkish coast.

A small but remarkable archaeological collection is housed in charming **Irinis Square**. Tables from the tavernas and cafeterias and a few bars spread out along the paved roads of the port, where you can relax while enjoying the sea which changes colour at twilight and the sailboats entering and leaving the harbour.

You will find fish tavernas on the left side of the port overlooking the small beach where you can taste the

Cosmopolitan Pythagorio

ΠΥΘΑΓΟΡΕΙΟ
PITHAGORIO
ΣΑΜΟΣ
SAMOS
ΑΕΡΟΔΡΟΜΙΟ - ΚΑΡΛΟΒΑΣΙ
AIRPORT - KARLOVASI
ΝΑΟΣ ΑΦΡΟΔΙΤΗΣ
TEMPLE OF APHRODITE
PARKING
ΠΛΗΡΟΦΟΡΙΕΣ
INFORMATION
ΚΑΣΤΡΟ
CASTLE
ΚΑΣΤΡΟ
CASTLE
N
W
E
S
ΤΡΑΠΕΖΑ BANK
1. ΑΣΤΥΝΟΜΙΑ POLICE
2. ΤΑΧΥΔΡΟΜΕΙΟ POST OFFICE
3. ΛΙΜΕΝΑΡΧΕΙΟ PORT AUTHORITY
4. ΔΗΜΑΡΧΕΙΟ TOWN HALL
5. ΑΡΧΑΙΟΛΟΓΙΚΟ ΜΟΥΣΕΙΟ ARGHEOLOGICAL MUSEUM
6. ΤΑΞΙ TAXI
7. Κ.Τ.Ε.Λ. BUS STATION
8. ΟΛΥΜΠΙΑΚΗ ΑΕΡΟΠΟΡΙΑ OLYMPIC AIRWAYS
9. ΑΓΑΛΜΑ ΠΥΘΑΓΟΡΑ STATUE OF PYTHAGORAS

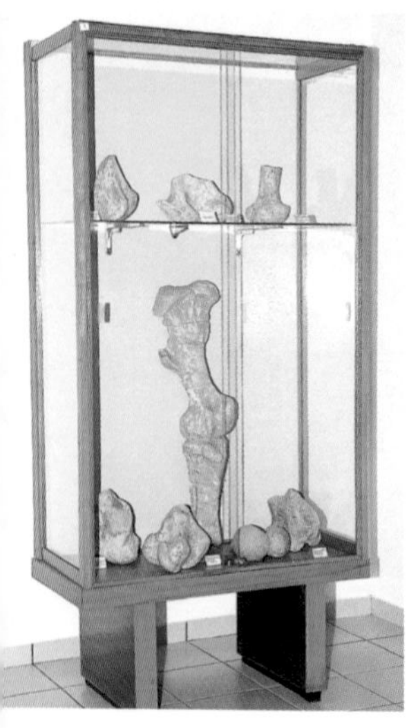

Exhibits in the Palaeontology Museum

fruits gathered from the sea.
There are three sites in the area that are worth visiting: the **Eupalinos tunnel,** the **Monastery of the Panagia Spiliani** and the **Kastro of Lycourgos Logothetis.**
Life began on the hillock where the Castle and the Church of Metamosphossi of Sotira are presently situated around the 4th millennium B.C. The Castle of Lycourgos Logothetis was built during the Revolution Period in 1821 using much material from ancient ruins. There is not much left of the Byzantium Castle that pre-existed, just a few relics have survived, including an inscription on the foundation dating back to 969 B.C. that informs us that Emperor Nikiforos renovated the Castle.
In one of the battles during the 1821 Revolution against the Turks, the Samians barricaded themselves in the Castle, thus this Castle constitutes a reminder for the inhabitants of the battles that were fought for freedom. Inside the Castle there are rooms, stairs and a steam bath that are still preserved.
On August 6th on the name-day of Sotira, a battle

between Greeks and Turks is celebrated - a battle that contributed to the liberation of Samos. This religious holiday is filled with many traditional ceremonial festivities, popular dances and swimming competitions. The end of the festivities is marked by setting fire to the 'enemy' flagship inside the harbour.

An uphill road leads from Pythagorio to the **Eupalinos tunnel** and to the Monastery of the Panagia Spiliani. A detour from here will take us to the remains of the ancient wall of **Polycrates.** Samos was also surrounded by a stone wall, as was the case with many other ancient cities. What remains relatively well preserved today of the solid 6,500 meter wall are the north-eastern and north-western sides of the wall.

After encircling the ancient city, the wall ended on the south side towards the beach. Traces of the wall that can be discerned by our inexperienced eye end at the road opposite **Tria Dontia** (three teeth), where three crumbling stone walls still stand, the remnants of an old Christian church.

Archaeological findings in Thermes

The serene beach at Glykorizo

You can read more about the historical facts of the Eupalinos tunnel on page 14-15.
The Monastery of the **Panagia Spiliani** is situated on the hill behind Pythagorio. The view from the small open area is impressive as our gaze caresses the Aegean all the way to the Turkish shores and from Pythagorio with the Kastro of Logothetis up to

The Kastro (Castle) of Logothetis

Heraion.
The small twin churches are dedicated to the Panagia (Virgin Mary) and to Ag. Georgios (St. George). Entering the cave we see in the depths of the cave a very old chapel-shrine.
The church is built at a depth of 94 steps from the cave's entrance. Three hand-made tanks collect the water that slowly drips from cracks in the rocks. The darkness together with the sound of the water dripping -which is the only sound heard inside this tranquil and

devout place- creates an especially emotional feeling for the visitor.
On the middle of the right wall of the small chapel is a built-in ancient ceramic icon of the "Esodia of Theotokou" (Harvest of the Virgin Mary), now broken and damaged by the passing of time and humidity.

"Polycratic Art" Among the most significant works of art from Antiquity

The Three Teeth

A legend tells us how the icon broke: "Many years ago some strangers came here out of devoutness by caique to secretly take the sacred icon back to their land, but the Virgin Mary did not want to leave Samos. So as they took the icon out of the caique it fell into the sea, breaking into five pieces. But the icon managed to return back to Samos where the Samians found it on the beach and returned it to the chapel. From that time it was also called 'Pa-nagia Kaliarmenissa' (Virgin Mary the Sailor) since it sailed on the sea like a boat and returned back home".

Panagia Spiliani, visitors undergo feelings of awe and devoutness here

In seems that the Virgin Mary's Cave has been a place for worship since ancient times, as can be seen from the remnants of vessels and pitchers from the 5th Century B.C. that have been found inside. It is also thought that the cave was a place of refuge for Pythagoras as well as the residence of the sibyl Phyto (a witch from antiquity).

Exhibited items in the Folkloric Museum

The coastal road that links Pythagorio and Heraion is the **ancient Iera Odos** (Sacred Road). It was said that way back in antiquity this road was adorned throughout its length with impressive statues of young lads and lasses.

Just before the detour to the settlement of Potokaki, we come across the **Doryssa Bay** Hotel situated inside the greater archaeological area of the region. There are two reasons why we mention this hotel: the first is the polymorphic building complex -the Chorio- which is a replica of a real 'chorio' or village, with the little houses having different architectural styles which represent various parts of Greece.

The second reason is the small but impressive "Nikolaos Dimitriou" Cultural Institute of Samos or Folkloric Museum, which is sited in the Chorio. Its exhibits characterise the agricultural life on the island mainly before the Second World War.

The Monastery of Panagia Spiliani

Coming out of the hotel we meet the junction to **Potokaki,** a beach that extends for many kilometres and which also has several hotels and tavernas.
The **ruins of Heraion** were discovered about 8 km from Pythagorio, which was the official sanctuary on Samos where it is said the goddess Hera grew up. The first temple, dated 8th Century B.C. was built of wood. According to mythology the first builders of the sanctuary were the Nymphs and the Leleges. Angeos, the king of Samos, built the wooden temple and installed an image of the goddess.
This first depiction of Hera was a piece of board with a painting of the goddess. It had great idolatry value so when the Samians discovered it, they tied it with wicker branches as they considered it sacrilege to touch it and carried it to the temple.

Column from the Temple of Polycrates in Heraion

Findings in the archaeological site of Heraion

In the 7th Century B.C. the wooden sanctuary was replaced by a construction made of stone which was destroyed by the Persian King Kyros. A few years later, the first huge temple was built on the site of the old ruins by the architect Roikos, which was also destroyed by the Persians. Finally, Polycrates assigned the task of building a new temple in the same place to Theodoros, the son of Roikos, which was described by the ancient historian Herodotus, as a splendid building. It had 133 columns and a height that reached 25 m.

This temple was destroyed by a geological disaster. What remains today is only one column which also gives its name to the region. After it was destroyed, various sanctuaries were continued to be built on this site (Heraion), followed later -with the spread of Christianity- by churches.:

Carefree moments and water-sports in Heraion and in Potokaki

View from beautiful Pythagorio

Pythagorio - Mavratzei - Pyrgos Marathokambos - Spatharei Pagondas

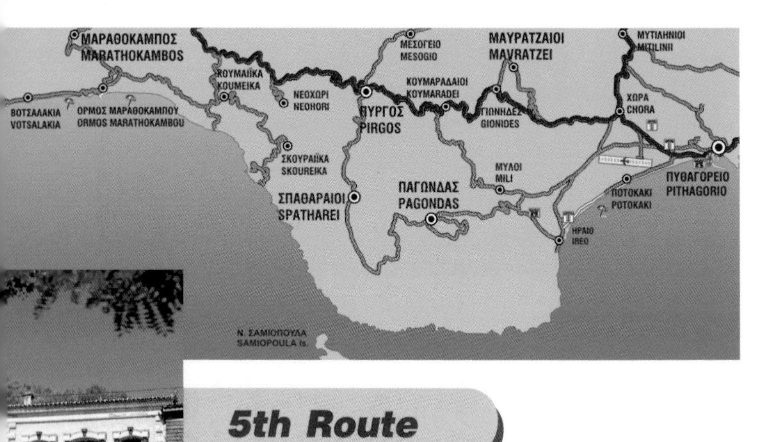

5th Route

Vathy or Pythagorio are the best starting points for us to get to know the **southern part of Samos.** We begin with a brief stroll along the forested slopes of Vournia and Pefkia and the small traditional villages that appear before us. At the end of our walk our weariness and the kilometres that we covered are rewarded with a dive into the cool waters of Marathokambos Bay, Votsalakia (with its pebbles) or the sandy beach of Psili Ammos (fine sand).

Leaving Pythagorio we follow the road to Chora - the old capital of the island. The plain that spreads out below the village is one of the largest on Samos and the most fertile.

Just after the junction leading to **Mavratzei** we meet the **Monastery of the Timios Stavros**, founded in

1592. In 1838 it was renovated and extended into the impressive and grand building that we see today.
Many of the relics that adorned the church and the monastery -and which are of unique value- have been moved to the **Ecclesiastical Museum** in Vathy where they can be seen and admired. The remarkable wood-carved iconostatis made in 1854 has remained in the church, covering the complete width of the church. Being of an equal height and vertical, this iconostatis is a masterpiece work of art due to the beauty, symmetry and harmony of its construction.
Our next stop is the village of Mavratzei, where the traditional arts of pottery and knitting still exist today, offering remarkable examples of these techniques.
In the centre of Samos we have **Koumaradeous,** one of the oldest villages on the island. About 1 km from the village is one of the largest monasteries on Samos, Megali Panagia, otherwise known as the **"Monastery with Five Houses".** The monastery was built in 1586 by the monks Nilos and Dionysios, while the Byzantine-

A potter at work

The Monasteries of Timios Stavros and Megali Panagia

styled catholic was erected in 1593.
The wall murals of the monastery have the same arrangement as that of the Monastery of Agios Oros. Of great value is the gold-plated wood-carved iconostasis with its ornamental relief birds, animals and plants.
During the years of the Greek Revolution in 1821 the Monastery gave refuge to Metropolitan Kyrillos, Lykourgos Logothetis and other local resistance fighters. This is also where the Samian resistance fighters also held their meetings.
Going towards Marathokambos we pass by **Pyrgos,** a village that produces honey, grapes and wine. Other renowned products from Pyrgos include hand-woven textile and woollen carpets.
From here you can travel either up to **Pandrosos** situated on Karkovouni Mountain or southwards to the village of **Spatharei** and continue on to the coastal

The coastal village of Pyrgos

village of **Limionaki.** Opposite us we can see the contours of the mystical islet of **Samiopoula** with its enchanting sandy beaches.
An idyllic place to take a break is **Koutsi** situated just below the main road. The spring with its crystallised water irrigates the dense forests and the nearby little taverna resembles an oasis in the heat of the summer months.
Continuing on the road to Marathokambos we come across a detour to **Platano,** a village with a picturesque shady square. Reaching **Ag. Theodoros** we turn left and then continue downhill towards the south-western shores of Samos.
Marathokambos is one of the large traditional villages of Samos with a long seashore that stretches for many kilometres along the western shores of the island. A significant source of money for the inhabitants of Marathokambos is the high quality soap and olive-oil that are produced here. The little harbour with its traditional shipyards is called Ormos and it has now

An icon of rare beauty at the Monastery of Megali Panagia

Multi-coloured caiques in the little port of Ormos Marathokambos

The village of Marathokambos

Soft sandy beaches and hours of relaxation in Psili Ammos and Limniona

Panoramic view of Pagondas

acquired a satisfactory infrastructure to host the thousands of tourists who arrive here every year to enjoy the picturesqueness of the region and the crystal-clear waters of the Aegean.

The plain of Marathokambos lies under the shadow of Mt. Fteria and ends at **Votsalakia beach,** which is one of the best on the island with its fine sand, transparent waters, attentive restaurants and tavernas situated over the waves, and all blend together to compose the picture you see.

A tap in the village of Platanos

Further west are the beaches of **Psili Ammos** (Fine Sand) and Chrisi Ammos (Golden Sand) which charm us and seduce us with their blue water and soft sand. At the end of the coastal road lies the bay of **Limniona.** From this point begins the scenic journey up the slopes of Mt. Kerkis, terminating at the attractive villages of **Kyriaki, Kallithea** and **Drakei.**

It is now time to return back. The distance from Marathokambos to Karlovasi is not more than 15 km so

many people prefer to return via Karlovasi in order to avoid the mountain journey.

If you prefer to remain faithful to your route you can turn towards **Koumeika** at Ormos and enjoy the refreshing coolness under the plane trees in the small squares. The small beach at Balos is perfect for those who prefer solitary swimming.

The road after Koumeika termi-nates at the village of **Skoureika** and the remote **Pefkos** beach. In order to return back, we again pass through Koumeika and from there we can choose to follow the passable dirt road that passes through **Neochori** and on to Koutsi and from there to the main road.

Votsalakia, one of the most beautiful beaches on the island

From Pyrgos we turn right to explore Spatharei and **Pagondas.** For the most part of the journey we have the company of high-trunked pine trees which allow us every now and then to see the blue-green waters and the contours of Samiopoula situated at the foot of the mountain.:

Skoureika and Koumeika

Neochori and Ormos Marathokambos.

92-93. Votsalakia Marathokambos

Samiopoula - Tsopela - Kyriakou Gaidouronissi - Kusantasi (Ephesus)

Excursions from Samos

Many small boats sail from the port of Pythagorio to the neighbouring deserted islets of Samiopoula and Gaidouronissi, to inaccessible and remote beaches, to Kusantasi in Turkey and to other islands in the Aegean, such as Patmos.
If you are planning to visit Kusantasi be sure and remember to have your passport with you. Be sure to check the time-table with the travel agencies because usually one trip a week is scheduled. The journey lasts less than 2 hours and you also have the opportunity to visit the ruins at Ancient Ephesus, one of the most powerful cities on the Asia Minor shores. The monuments of the town

are quite well-preserved and overawe visitors with their grandeur.

One excursion that is a must is to the **islet of Samiopoula** and if possible, not during the high tourist season, as you can then feel as if you are the first person to touch the white sandy beach and the blue waters.

But even when it is crowded, this small beach is charming and worth the visit. Be sure to supply yourself with water and fruit or a sandwich, while there is a small taverna below the **Chapel of Ag. Pelagia** that serves fish and roasted meat.

The remaining excursions to the beaches at **Gaidouronissi, Psili Ammos, Tsopela** and **Kyriakou** offer the same opportunities to get to know Samos and to enjoy an adventurous day, since most of these excursions are accompanied by a picnic organised by the captain.

95-97 Samiopoula. You... white sand and amazing waters

Ikaria

PROLOGUE

The 297 km2 that is the area of the hilly island of Ikaria situated in the Aegean Sea hide several impressive beaches, scenic villages with intense local colour, customs, the mountainous volume of Atheras with its unique charm and natural hot springs, which until the past decade was the reason why Ikaria had become known. In continuation, the island was 'discovered' by the first wave of tourists who respected the island's natural beauty and virgin land.

The island has a population of around 7,000 inhabitants and 60 settlements and villages. Customs

Agios Kirikos

The attractive beach at Na

and traditions are still maintained throughout 'Nikaria' -as it is called by the locals- and the locals do not look at tourism as a profession. For this reason the hospitality that they offer the visitor is warm and kind-hearted, and in combination with the impressive natural environment, Ikaria wins our hearts.

MYTHOLOGY - HISTORY

The name of Ikaria is closely related to Greek mythology and the reckless **Icarus, son of Daedalus.**
Daedalus, an exceptional architect and statuesque, lived in the palace of Minos in Knossos together with his wife and son Icarus. Among his works were the construction of the palaces and the renowned Labyrinth, where the Minotaur lived.
Minos, enthusiastic over the works of Daedalus, did not allow him to leave the island as he was afraid that Daedalus might go and work in some other city and build a palace that would be more grand than Knossos. Thus the ever-engineer Daedalus constructed a

prototype machine with wings from bird feathers stuck together with wax, which allowed him to fly. He taught his son the secrets of flying and they left together, flying to Crete.
Young Icarus became captivated with the sensation of flying and flew away from his father towards the sun. The heat melted his wings and he fell into the sea and drowned, thus giving his name to the island and to the Icarian Sea.
Information con-cerning the history of Ikaria during the period of Antiquity is scarce. The island was inhabited by the Ions towards the end of the 9th Century B.C., by the Venetians in the 13th C. and later by the Turks. In 1835 the island joined with Leros, Kalymnos and Patmos to form the 'Tetra-island' until 1912 when it was incorporated with the rest of Greece.

GETTING TO KNOW IKARIA

Until a few years ago Ikaria was known only for its **hot springs,** but in recent years more and more young

The beach at Armenisti

people are discovering its natural beauties and crystal-clear waters.

Gialiskari, an endless beach next to the warm waters of the Aegean

Another characteristic is the idiomorphic relationship the inhabitants of the island have with time. There are villages where the 'oven' only opens after 2.00 p.m. and you will therefore have to be very patient while waiting to be served at the tavernas. But this does not dissatisfy the well-disposed visitor; on the contrary, this helps him to harmonise with the relaxing rhythms and enjoy his carefree vacation.

The ship anchors in **Agios Kirikos,** the capital of Ikaria, where the Neo-Classical building housing the police and the port authority dominates. You will find the most significant hot springs in the area of **Therma,** where remnants of ancient baths have also been discovered.

There are a number of choices to go swimming, such as the beach at **Agios Kirikos** and many others all along the coast, where you can go either on foot or by caique. On the road to **Armenisti** we will meet the scenic villages of **Mavrato, Oxea and Mileopo,** built

The picturesque village of Evdilos

high up on the hills with rich vegetation.

Evdilos is the second harbour on the island, with narrow roads, flowered yards and attractive beaches. You will find the small villages of **Mesaria, Akamatra, Dafni, Steli and Petropouli** perched along the ridge of the hill - all offering a unique view of the sea. You can see the **Kastro of Nikarias** overlooking the village of **Kosikia,** which is a Byzantine fort dating back to the 10th C. In Kambos there are the ruins of Ancient **Inois** and the Archaelogical Museum with findings from the ancient city.

The sandy beach at **Gialiskari** attracts quite a few tourists who stay either in the settlement or in the surrounding villages. Armenisti has developed into a tourist resort for the young who are bewitched by the natural beauty of the beach at **Na.** The road climbs up to the mountain village of **Christos of Rachon,** a green-filled region until the last forest fire in 1993. Large festivals are held on the name-days of the Monastery of the Panagias of Evangelistrias on August 15th and the 'Metamorphosis of Sotira' on August 6th where the whole island takes part.

Fourni

There is an island chain between Ikaria and Samos known as **Fourni** which welcomes its few visitors. In the picturesque harbour you will find the night-life centred among the fish-taverns that grill fish that come directly from the nets and the kafenia filled with locals who are always willing to tell you their tales.

The beaches both at inhabited Fourni and **Thimena** and on the adjacent uninhabited islets are attractive and quiet. You can sail from the harbour to the opposite Cove of **Chrisomilia** by caique. As for the remaining distances, you can walk since there are no cars on the island.

View from Fourni

Ephesus was one of the most significant cities in Antiquity. It was built on the western shores of Asia Minor opposite Samos, in the estuary of the ancient Kaistros River where a small cove was formed. During its period of acme the city was situated next to the sea, but with the passing of eons the deposits (silt) from the river created a narrow strip of land, so today the visitor will visit ancient Ephesus which lies about 8 km inland from the sea.
Ephesus and the notable **Sanctuary of Artemidos** are mentioned in detail in many sources of antiquity. According to mythology the Amazons were the founders of Ephesus, while historical sources mention that the Kares, the Leleges and the Lydous were among the first settlers.
Every summer thousands of visitors arrive from Greece and Turkey to visit Ephesus, they walk around the well-preserved ancient roads and gaze with wonder at the monuments of Antiquity. Let us give you a brief guide through the major sites.

The monuments

Ephesus has been inhabited for many centuries now so therefore only the last phases of many of the monuments have been saved. Small sections of the Ancient, Classical and Hellenistic buildings have remained, but some however are quite impressive and overwhelm us when we first look at them.
The Sanctuary of Artemida was one of the

'ornaments' during the period of acme of some of the greatest artists in ancient times. Only some remnants of the temple that was situated between the hills of **Panaeir Dag and Agiasolouk** exist today, including the sculptured adornments of pillars and capitals that are today exibited in the British Museum.

As for the Post-Classical temple that was built in 356 B.C. after the previous one had been destroyed by fire, only a column has been preserved, and a part of this has been restored by Austrian archaeologists.

The **Temple of Hadrian** was build around 127 A.D. and was later dedicated to the Emperors Galerio, Maximiano, Dioclitiano and Constantio Chloro. This monument regained its old splendour after being restored.

There is a very long list of notable monuments at

Ephesus. The **public market** with the **small conservatory**, the baths, the prytaneum and the temples of Rome and Caesar, together with a **tri-aisled bacilica** that was constructed along the north side - all give us a feeling of the life at Ephesus during the Roman period. Various historical phases of the city are portrayed at the **theatre at Ephesus**. The stage is unusually large but it was continuously being changed and rebuilt between the 1st and 2nd Century A.D. During the following period the audience's gallery took its final form, seating about 30,000 persons. The last repair work was carried out around the 3rd C. during the period of Karakallas.

The Library in Celsius

On of the more impressive monuments is **Celsiu's library.** Basically it was not originally a library but rather a huge war memorial containing a tomb with a sarcophagus built by Akylas in memory of his father. But in later times it was transformed into a library with the capacity to store around 12,000 papyruses. The four female statues that adorn the façade of the restored library represent the Virtue (Areti), the Knowledge (Episteme), the Sagacity (Sophia) and the Fortune (Evnia) Celsiu.

The Temple of Handrian

Hot springs, gymnasiums and stadiums existed then in various parts of the city, as well as water works and fountains - an example being Tryanou which has been restored. Luxurious houses and Christian monuments supplement the findings in Ephesus.

Ν. ΣΑΜΟΣ
SAMOS IS.

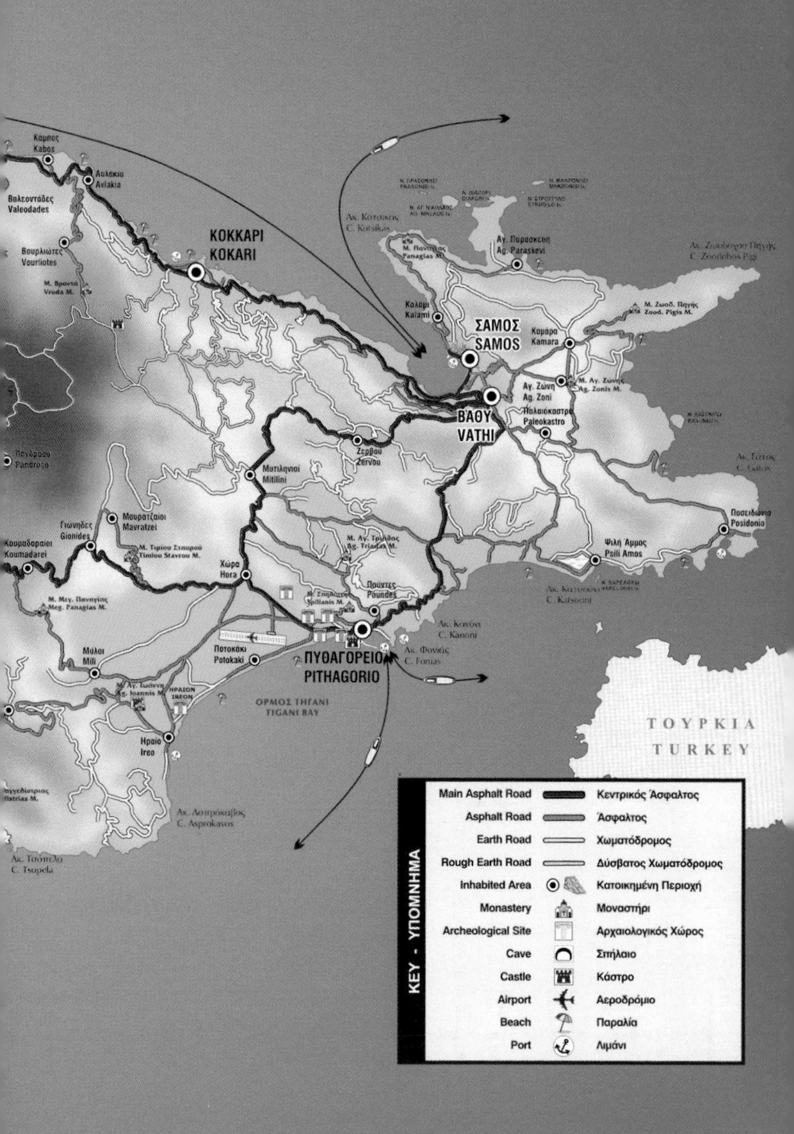

Κάμπος
Kabos
Αυλάκια
Avlakia
Βαλεοντάδες
Valeodades
Βουρλιώτες
Vourliotes
ΚΟΚΚΑΡΙ
KOKARI
Ακ. Κοτσικας
C. Kotsikas
Αγ. Παρασκευη
Ag. Paraskevi
Ακ. Ζωοδοχου Πηγής
C. Zoodohos Pigi
Καλάμι
Kalami
ΣΑΜΟΣ
SAMOS
Καμαρα
Kamara
Μ. Ζωοδ. Πηγής
Zood. Pigis M.
Αγ. Ζώνη
Ag. Zoni
Μ. Αγ. Ζώνης
Ag. Zonis M.
ΒΑΘΥ
VATHI
Παλαιόκαστρο
Paleokastro
Ζερβού
Zervou
Πάνδροσο
Pandroso
Μυτιληνιοί
Mitilini
Ακ. Γάτος
C. Gatos
Μαυρατζαίοι
Mavratzei
Γιωνίδες
Gionides
Μ. Τιμίου Σταυρού
Timiou Stavrou M.
Κουμαδαραίοι
Koumadarei
Χώρα
Hora
Μ. Αγ. Τριάδας
Ag. Triadas M.
Πουντες
Poundes
Ποσειδώνιο
Posidonio
Ψιλή Άμμος
Psili Amos
Ακ. Κατσούνι
C. Katsouni
Μ. Μεγ. Παναγίας
Meg. Panagias M.
Ακ. Κανόνι
C. Kanoni
Μύλοι
Mili
Ποτοκάκι
Potokaki
ΠΥΘΑΓΟΡΕΙΟ
PITHAGORIO
Ακ. Φονιάς
C. Fonias
ΗΡΑΙΟΝ
IREON
ΟΡΜΟΣ ΤΗΓΑΝΙ
TIGANI BAY
ΤΟΥΡΚΙΑ
TURKEY
Ηραίο
Ireo
Ακ. Ασπρόκαβος
C. Asprokavos
Ακ. Τσόπελα
C. Tsopela
KEY - ΥΠΟΜΝΗΜΑ
Main Asphalt Road — Κεντρικός Άσφαλτος
Asphalt Road — Άσφαλτος
Earth Road — Χωματόδρομος
Rough Earth Road — Δύσβατος Χωματόδρομος
Inhabited Area — Κατοικημένη Περιοχή
Monastery — Μοναστήρι
Archeological Site — Αρχαιολογικός Χώρος
Cave — Σπήλαιο
Castle — Κάστρο
Airport — Αεροδρόμιο
Beach — Παραλία
Port — Λιμάνι

HOTELS

ΑΓ. ΚΩΝΣΤΑΝΤΙΝΟΣ / AG. KONSTANTINOS

ΔΑΦΝΗ / DAFNI	22730.94003
ΗΡΩ / IRO	22730.94013
ΑΓ. ΚΩΝΣΤΑΝΤΙΝΟΣ / AG. KONSTANTINOS	22730.94000
APOLLONIA BAY	22730.94444
ΑΡΙΑΔΝΗ / ARIADNI	22730.94205
ΑΤΛΑΝΤΙΣ / ATLANTIS	22730.94329

ΑΛΥΚΕΣ-ΜΥΚΑΛΗ / ALYKES-MYKALI

SAINT NIKOLAS OF SAMOS	22730.25230

ΑΥΛΑΚΙΑ / AVLAKIA

ΑΥΛΑΚΙΑ / AVLAKIA	22730.94230

ΗΡΑΙΟΝ / IREON

ΑΔΑΜΑΝΤΙΑ / ADAMANTIA	22730.95288
ΑΚΤΗ ΗΡΑΙΟΥ / AKTI IREOU	22730.95326
ΑΝΑΤΟΛΗ / ANATOLI	22730.95369
ΑΓΓΕΛΙΚΗ / ANGELIKI	22730.95335
PARIS BEACH	22730.95397
ΡΑΝΙΑ / RANIA	22730.91506
ΣΠΙΤΙ / SPITI	22730.95346
ΒΕΝΕΤΙΑ / VENETIA	22730.95295
ΑΛΕΞΑΝΔΡΟΣ / ALEXANDROS	22730.95293
ΦΑΡΟΣ / FAROS	22730.95262
HERA	22730.61180
ΝΙΚΗ / NIKI	22730.95336
ΚΟΧΥΛΙ / KOCHYLI	22730.95282

ΚΑΛΑΜΙ / KALAMI

ΑΝΘΕΜΙΣ / ANTHEMIS	22730.28060
IONIA MARIS	22730.28428
INO	22730.23241
KIRKI BEACH	22730.23030
LA PISCINE	.
ΜΥΡΙΝΗ / MIRINI	22730.28452
ΑΙΓΑΙΟΝ / AEGEON	22730.22838
ΑΝΔΡΟΜΕΔΑ / ANDROMEDA	22730.22925
IRESSIONI	22730.24523
ΚΛΕΟΜΕΝΗΣ / KLEOMENIS	22730.23232
ΜΕΛΑΜΦΥΛΟ / MELAMFYLO	22730.22126
ΝΟΤΗΣ / NOTIS	22730.22722
ΠΑΝΘΕΑ / PANTHEA	22730.22275
ΠΛΟΥΤΑΡΧΟΣ / PLOUTARHOS	22730.23440
ΠΥΘΑΓΟΡΑΣ / PYTHAGORAS	22730.28422
ΣΚΟΡΠΙΟΣ / SCORPIOS	22730.22600
VILLA PANORAMA	22730.28151
BELLA VISTA	22730.27660

ΚΑΜΠΟΣ ΒΟΥΡΛΙΩΤΩΝ / KAMBOS VOURLIOTON

ΑΓΝΑΝΤΙ / AGNANTI	22730.94087

ΚΑΡΛΟΒΑΣΙ / KARLOVASI

SAMENA INN	22730.35445
SAMENA MEZONETES	22730.34988
ΑΙΓΑΙΟΝ / AEGEON	22730.33466
ΑΜΑΝΤΑ / AMANDA	22730.35230
ΑΣΠΑΣΙΑ / ASPASSIA	22730.30201
ΜΕΡΩΠΗ / MEROPI	22730.32510
SAMENA BAY	22730.30811
SAMENA PORT	22730.34527

ΚΑΡΛΟΒΑΣΙ / KARLOVASI

ΑΝΕΜΑ	22730.30500
ΕΡΑΤΩ / ERATO	22730.34600
ΕΣΠΕΡΙΑ / ESPERIA	22730.30706
ΝΕΦΕΛΗ / NEFELI	22730.34000
ΑΣΤΗΡ / ASTIR	22730.33150

ΚΑΤΣΟΥΝΙ / KATSOUNI

ARES	.

ΚΕΡΒΕΛΙ / KERVELI

KERVELI'S VILLAGE	22730.23006

ΚΟΚΑΡΙ / KOKARI

ΑΡΙΟΝ / ARION	22730.92020
ARMONIA BAY	22730.92279
KOKKARI BEACH	22730.92263
OLYMPIA VILLAGE	22730.92420
ΠΑΝΟΡΑΜΑ / PANORAMA	22730.92444
AMYRSONIS	.
ANGELA - CHRISTINA	.
ΑΣΤΕΡΙΑΣ / ASTERIAS	
ΑΘΗΝΑ / ATHINA	22730.92030
ΔΗΜΗΤΡΑ / DIMITRA	22730.92300
ΕΛΕΝΗ-ΓΙΟΛΑΝΤΑ / ELENI-GIOLANDA	22730.92025
ΦΡΥΝΗ / FRYNI	22730.92360
ΓΑΛΗΝΗ / GALINI	22730.92331
GOLDEN SUN	22730.92161
KALYDON	22730.92605
ΛΑΙΜΟΣ / LEMOS	22730.92250
OLYMPIA BEACH	22730.92353
SUN RISE BEACH	22730.92447
ΤΣΑΜΑΔΟΥ / TSAMADOU	22730.92240
VENUS	22730.92230
VILLA MARIA	22730.92085
VILLES ARCHANGELOS	22730.92135
ΛΗΤΩ / LITO	22730.92207
ΑΝΤΖΕΛΑ / ANTZELA	22730.92351
BLUE SEA	22730.92307
BLUE SKY	22730.92387
KOKKARI - PENELOPE	22730.92382
ΛΕΜΟΝΑΚΙΑ / LEMONAKIA	22730.92357
ΠΟΣΕΙΔΩΝ / POSIDON	22730.92384

ΜΑΛΑΓΡΙ / MALAGRI

ΠΟΣΕΙΔΩΝ / POSIDON	22730.37202

ΜΑΡΑΘΟΚΑΜΠΟΣ / MARATHOKAMBOS

KERKIS BAY	22730.37202
ΟΡΦΕΑΣ / ORFEAS	22730.37185
AGRILIONAS BEACH	22730.37379
ΑΛΕΞΑΝΔΡΑ / ALEXANDRA	22730.37419
ANTHEMIS VILLAGE	22730.37185
HERMES	22730.37347
LIMNIONA VILLAGE	22730.37274
LIMNIONAS BAY	22730.37057
MARY	22730.37006
ΝΗΡΗΙΔΕΣ / NIRIIDES	.
OCEANIS	22730.37333
ΠΕΛΑΓΟΣ / PELAGOS	22730.37006
ΣΜΑΡΑΓΔΑ / SMARAGDA	22730.37017

ΜΑΡΑΘΟΚΑΜΠΟΣ / MARATHOKAMBOS

ΣΟΦΗ / SOFI	22730.37035
ΧΡΥΣΟΠΕΤΡΟ / CHRYSSOPETRO	22730.37247
VILLA FLORA	22730.37434
VOTSALAKIA PLAGE	22730.37355

ΜΕΣΟΚΑΜΠΟΣ / MESSOKAMBOS

OCEANIDA BAY	22730.61620

ΠΕΥΚΑΚΙΑ / PEFKAKIA

ΠΛΑΚΑ / PLAKA	22730.23725

ΠΥΡΓΟΣ / PIRGOS

KOUTSI	22730.61389

ΠΥΘΑΓΟΡΕΙΟ / PITHAGORIO

PROTEAS BAY	22730.62144
DORYSSA BAY	22730.61360
FITO BUNGALOWS HOTEL	22730.61314
MARITSA'S BAY	22730.61016
SAMOS SUN	22730.61791
ΤΑΡΣΑΝΑΣ / TARSANAS	22730.61210
ΑΝΘΕΜΟΥΣΑ / ANTHEMOUSSA	22730.61680
ΑΝΤΩΝΙΟΣ / ANTONIOS	22730.61002
ΑΠΟΛΩΝ / APOLLON	22730.61683
ΑΡΓΩ / ARGO	.
ASTRA VILLAGE	22730.61752
ΑΘΗΝΑΪΣ / ATHINAIS	22730.91378
ΑΘΩΣ / ATHOS	22730.61847
BELVEDERE	22730.61218
DAMO	22730.61303
DOLPHIN	22730.61205
ΝΤΟΡΑ / DORA	22730.61456
ΕΥΠΑΛΗΝΙΟ / EFPALINIO	22730.61466
ΕΒΕΛΙΝ / EVELIN	22730.61124
ΦΡΟΣΩ / FROSSO	22730.61559
Γ. ΣΑΝΔΑΛΗΣ / G. SANDALIS	22730.61691
GLIKORIZA BEACH	22730.61321
HERA	22730.61319
HERA II	22730.61319
ΗΛΙΟΣ / ILIOS	22730.61365
ΚΑΚΤΟΣ / KAKTOS	22730.61284
ΚΑΣΤΕΛΙ / KASTELI	22730.61728
ΚΟΥΡΟΣ / KOUROS	22730.61611
LABITO	22730.61086
LABITO II	22730.61086
LENOX	22730.61709
MARIONA	22730.61210
ΜΕΛΑΝΘΕΜΟΣ / MELANTHEMOS	22730.61554
ΜΥΚΑΛΗ / MYKALI	22730.61110
NEA IONIA	22730.61449
PEGASUS	22730.61455
ΠΟΛΥΚΡΑΤΗΣ / POLYCRATES	22730.61398
ΠΟΛΥΞΕΝΗ / POLYXENI	22730.61590
PRINCESSA	22730.62381
ΠΥΘΑΓΟΡΑΣ / PYTHAGORAS	22730.61373
PYTHAIS	22730.61526
REMEZZO	22730.61120
ΣΑΜΑ / SAMA	22730.61123
ΣΑΜΕΝΑ / SAMENA	22730.61024
ΣΑΜΙΟΠΟΥΛΑ / SAMIOPOULA	22730.61824
SILENA	22730.62675

ΠΥΘΑΓΟΡΕΙΟ / PITHAGORIO

SILENA	22730.62675
ΣΤΡΑΤΟΣ / STRATOS	22730.61157
ΖΕΦΥΡΟΣ / ZEFYROS	22730.61359
ΖΟΡΜΠΑΣ / ZORBAS	22730.61009
ΑΛΕΞΑΝΔΡΑ / ALEXANDRA	22730.61429
ΕΛΠΙΣ / ELPIS	22730.61144
EVRIPILI	22730.61834
ΟΛΥΜΠΙΑΔΑ / OLYMPIADA	22730.61490
PARIS	22730.61513
VILLA MOUSTAKAS	22730.61444

ΠΟΤΟΚΑΚΙ / POTOKAKI

BONZAI	.
CHRIS BUNGALOWS	22730.61607
HYDRELE BEACH	22730.61702
ΑΡΕΤΟΥΣΑ / ARETHOUSSA	22730.61616
EL CORAL	22730.61604
ENTRIOU-N	22730.61702
ΚΑΤΕΡΙΝΑ / KATERINA	22730.61963
ΠΗΝΕΛΟΠΗ / PENELOPE	22730.61601
ΠΟΤΟΚΑΚΙ / POTOKAKI	22730.61339
ΒΙΚΤΩΡΙΑ / VICTORIA	22730.61606
ΜΑΡΙΤΣΑ / MARITSA	22730.62130

ΣΑΜΟΣ (χώρα) - SAMOS (town)

ΑΚΡΟΠΟΛΙΣ / ACROPOLIS	22730.27604
ΑΝΘΟΥΣΑ / ANTHOUSSA	22730.24423
ΕΜΙΛΥ / EMILY	22730.24691
ΓΚΑΛΑΞΙ / GALAXY	22730.22665
GOLDEN SUN	22730.24300
ΚΕΔΡΟΣ / KEDROS	22730.80088
ΚΡΙΤΩΝ / KRITON	22730.23156
LA MIRAGE	22730.23868
MATINA	22730.95223
ΤΟΥΛΑ / TOULA	22730.27644
ZODIAC	22730.27574
ΑΡΤΕΜΙΣ / ARTEMIS	22730.27792
ΜΑΚΡΥΣ / MAKRIS	22730.22675

ΒΑΛΕΟΝΤΑΔΕΣ / VALEONTADES

ΑΗΔΟΝΟΚΑΣΤΡΟ / AIDONOKASTRO	22730.94686

ΒΑΘΥ / VATHI

ΑΙΟΛΙΣ / AEOLIS	22730.28904
ΧΡΙΣΤΙΑΝΑ / CHRISTIANA	22730.23084
ENNEA MOUSSES	22730.23971
SIRINES BEACH	22730.24666
VIRTZINIA	22730.27819
BONI	22730.28790
DIANA	22730.23921
HELEN	22730.28215
IRINNA	
ΟΔΥΣΣΕΑΣ / ODYSSEAS	22730.27846
ΠΑΡΑΔΕΙΣΟΣ / PARADISSOS	22730.23911
PHYLLIS	22730.23624
ΣΑΜΟΣ / SAMOS	22730.28377
SIBYLA	22730.23396
ΒΑΘΥ / VATHY	22730.28124
GRACELAND	22730.27504
ΛΑΣΚΑΡΗΣ / LASKARIS	22730.27679
ΜΕΔΟΥΣΑ / MEDOUSSA	22730.23501

USEFUL INFORMATIONS

ΜΟΥΣΕΙΑ		MUSEUMS
Αρχαιολογικό Σάμου	22730.27469	Samos Archaeological
Λαογραφικό Καρλοβασίου	-	Karlovasi Folklore Museum
Παλαιοντολογικό Μυτιληνιοί	22730.52055	Paleontologic Museum Mitilini
Λαογραφικό Πυθαγορείου	22730.87729	Pithagorio Folklore Museum
Αρχαιολογικό Πυθαγορείου	-	Pithagorio Archaeological
Εκκλησιαστικό & Βυζαντινό	22730.27312	Samos Byzantine Museum
ΑΣΤΥΝΟΜΙΑ		**POLICE**
Σάμου	22730.27980	Samos
Καρλοβασίου	22730.32444	Karlovasi
Μαραθοκάμπου	22730.31222	Marathokabos
Πυθαγορείου	22730.61100	Pithagorio
ΛΙΜΕΝΑΡΧΕΙΑ		**PORT AUTHORITY**
Σάμου	22730.27318	Samos
Καρλοβασίου	22730.32343	Karlovasi
Πυθαγορείου	22730.61225	Pithagorio
Πειραιά	210.4226000	Piraeus
ΝΟΣΟΚΟΜΕΙΟ	22730.27426	**HOSPITAL**
Σάμου	22730.24601	Samos
ΚΕΝΤΡΟ ΥΓΕΙΑΣ	22730.32222	**HEALTH CENTRE**
Καρλοβασίου	22730.32266	Karlovasi
ΤΟΥΡΙΣΤΙΚΗ ΑΣΤΥΝΟΜΙΑ		**TOURIST POLICE**
Σάμος	22730.27404	Samos
ΝΟΜΑΡΧΙΑ		**PREFECTURE**
Σάμος	22730.80000-7	Samos
ΠΥΡΟΣΒΕΣΤΙΚΗ		**FIRE DEPARTMENT**
Σάμος	199	Samos
ΚΤΕΛ		**BUS STATION**
Σάμος	22730.27262	Samos
ΤΑΞΙ		**TAXI**
Σάμος	22730.28404	Samos
Καρλόβασι	22730.32659	Karlovasi
Μαραθόκαμπος	22730.31000	Marathokabos
Κάμπος Μαραθοκάμπου	22730.37600	Kabos Marathokabos
Πυθαγόρειο	22730.61450	Pithagorio
ΑΕΡΟΔΡΟΜΙΟ		**AIRPORT**
Σάμος	22730.61555	Samos
ΟΛΥΜΠΙΑΚΗ		**OLYMPIC AIRWAYS**
Σάμος	22730.27237	Samos
Ε.Ο.Τ.		**ORGANIZATION TOURISM**
Σάμος	22730.28530	Samos
ΟΔΙΚΗ ΒΟΗΘΕΙΑ		**ROAD ASSISTANCE**
ΕΛΠΑ	22730.27104	ELPA
EXPRESS SERVICE	22730.25158	EXPRESS SERVICE
INTERAMERICAN	22730.23330	INTERAMERICAN